PREGNANCY COOKBOOK

90 Recipes Ready Within 30 Minutes

MELANIE

ISBN: 9781520895376

Are you looking for recipes that are not only healthy but also easy to follow? You are moms-to-be or just a cooking lover or even just an eating lover? This Pregnancy Cookbook is the one for you to learn and follow, so what are else in this book? With the main goal of creating a well-balanced diet for pregnancy, this is a collection of healthy recipes that are packed with a lot of nutrients, so this is the cookbook that every pregnancy should have.

In addition, it contains 15 chapters within 90 recipes named the main ingredient included in those recipes. You are easy to find the recipes you are looking for according to the name of main ingredients, also the name of each chapter.

For example, in chapter 1, you will see a collection of 6 tasty recipes for beef and all of them are really healthy and mouth-watering. Colorful and crunchy are two adjectives to describe the chapter of salad. With the chapter of smoothies, they will be irresistible to everybody. Especially all recipes contained in this book come with step-by-step instructions which make them become more simple and easier for everybody to follow, even the beginners.

Moreover, unlike other similar cookbooks, "PREGNANCY COOKBOOK: 90 Recipes Ready within 30 Minutes" gets you to start on the DASH Diet right away without spending hours in the kitchen or reading "theories".

And much more!

And here is what this book contains:

Contents

Introduction

During pregnancy your body needs an extra amount of all nutrients and mineral for the healthy development of both mom-to-be and your baby. Plus, the foods you eat will be also the main source to nourish your baby during this time. Therefore, a healthy diet plays an important role in providing an adequate nutrition to both of you and baby because a well-balance-diet can help you meet your nutritional need without taking any vitamin supplements.

Knowing the importance of a healthy balanced-diet during pregnancy, this book is a collection of healthy recipes which are as easy and quick as possible for moms-to-be to follow at home. But what are else as special things included in this small e-book? All the recipes recommended in this book focus on the fresh and healthy ingredients, which is aimed to avoid the processed foods and high-fat foods, especially, most of them won't include too much ingredients and won't take you much time to make, just within 30 minutes or less spending in the kitchen for each recipe to be completely made, you already have a tasty meal for yourself or for your family. I hope that this book will inspire the busy women who often consider doing cooking is just something like a daunting job get into the kitchen more often.

Chapter 1. Beef

Due to the higher need of iron for the healthy development of baby during pregnancy, beef becomes the great source for iron that pregnancy should add to meals more often. A pregnant woman is recommended to take 30 mg of iron per day and with 3 ounces of lean beef, it will give you 3.2 mg of iron, so eat beef every day is a natural way to get sufficiency of iron. Let's add these tasty beef recipes to the list of your healthy diet.

1.Tenderloin Steak

Serving: 4

Total time: 30 minutes

Ingredients:

- 4 beef tenderloin steak – 6 ounces of each steak

- Sliced mushroom (fresh) – 1 cup

- Reduced-sodium broth – ½ cup

- Steak seasoning – 1 teaspoon

- Butter – 2 tablespoons

- Heavy whipping cream – ¼ cup

- Steak sauce – 1 tablespoon

- Garlic salt with parsley – 1 teaspoon

- Minced chives – 1 teaspoon

Instructions:

- Season the steak with steak seasoning.

- Melt the butter in a large skillet over medium heat, place the steak and cook about 5 minutes for each side of steak. Take the steaks out of the skillet.

- Putting the mushrooms to the skillet and cook it until tender, then add the broth and stir well.

- Add cream, steak sauce and garlic salt, then stir them well. Continue to cook until the sauce is slightly thickened.

- Return the steak to the sauce, turn to coat and heat through. Add minced chives and stir. Serve.

2.Beef Stir Fry With Broccoli and Bean

Serving: 4

Total time: 20 minutes

Ingredients:

- Beef (cut into thin strips) – 1 pound

- Broccoli – 8 ounces (3 florets)

- Cannellini beans – 1 can (15 ounces)

- Reduced-sodium soy sauce – 2 teaspoons

- Orange juice – ¼ cup

- Carrot (cut into thin slices) – 2

- Crushed red pepper – ¼ teaspoon

- Fresh Ginger (chopped) – 1 teaspoon

- Garlic (minced) – 2 cloves

- Vegetable oil – 2 teaspoons

- Green onion (cut into long thin strips) – 6

Instructions:

- Heat one teaspoon of vegetable oil in a large skillet over medium heat, then add beef, garlic and ginger to the skillet and stir them well until the beef turns brown (about 3 minutes). Remove all from the skillet and put them in a bowl.

- Add carrots and broccoli to the skillet with the remaining oil. Cook and stir for 3 minutes, then add green onions to the mixture and cook 1 minute more.

- Pour orange juice, soy sauce and crushed red pepper then toss to coat.

- Return the beef to the skillet and add beans, then cook until the beans are tender, then serve.

3.Asparagus Beef Stir Fry

Serving: 4

Total time: 30 minutes

Ingredients:

- Beef tenderloin roast (cubed) – 1 pound

- Asparagus (cut in to 2 inch pieces) – 1 pound

- Fresh mushroom (sliced) – ½ pound

- Green onion (sliced) – 1

- Salt – ½ teaspoon

- Pepper – ¼ teaspoon

- Canola oil – 1 teaspoon

- Garlic (minced) – 2 cloves

- Butter – ¼ cup

- Reduced-sodium soy sauce – 1 teaspoon

- Lemon juice – ½ teaspoon

Instructions:

- Heat the oil in a large skillet. Add beef, onion, salt and pepper, cook and stir for 5 minutes. Add garlic and stir 1 minute more. Remove all from the skillet.

- Add asparagus and mushrooms and butter to the skillet with the remaining oil and cook and stir well until all the ingredients are tender.

- Then add the cooked beef to mixture of asparagus and mushroom and stir in soy sauce and lemon juice. Heat all the ingredients through.

- Then serve with rice.

4.Grilled Beef

Serving: 4

Total time: 30 minutes

Ingredients:

- 4 rib-eye steaks (trimmed) – 8 ounces for each (¾ inch thick)

- Extra-virgin olive oil – 8 teaspoons

- Salt – 4 teaspoons

- Pepper – 2 teaspoons

Instructions:

- Preheat your grill on high heat to allow it to become very hot.

- Using 2 teaspoons olive oil (1 teaspoon for each side), ½ teaspoon of pepper and 1 teaspoon of salt to season for each steak and season both sides.

- Place steak on the grill and let it sit for about 4 minutes, when the steak turns brown, turn over to the other side and continue to cook about 3 minutes to get medium rare.

- It's done.

Tips:

- Let steaks sit at room temperature for 30 minutes before cooking to help it cook more evenly.

- The cooking time will depend on how thick the steaks are.

- To know how you like your steaks, just gently push in fleshly part under the thumb for a rare steak, push slightly under rare point for medium rare, push half way down fleshy part of thumb for medium and slop down towards dent in wrist and push just before you hit bone for medium-medium-good steaks.

5.Beef Onion Stir Fry

Serving: 2

Total time: 30 minutes

Ingredients:

- Bottom around steak (thinly sliced) – 1 pound

- Red onion (thinly sliced) – 1

- Lemon juice – 6 tablespoons

- Water – ¼ cup

- Soy sauce – ¼ cup

- Black pepper – 1 teaspoon

- Cooking oil – 8 tablespoons

Instructions:

- Add soy sauce, lemon juice and pepper and beef in a large bowl and let it marinate for 15 minutes.

- Heat oil in a large pan over medium heat. Put the beef and cook and turn the sides of beef for 10 minutes, then add the onion slices, stir well.

- Serve.

6.Beef Steak With Garlic Soy Sauce

Serving: 2

Total time: 20 minutes

Ingredients:

- Beef chuck (cut into 3 large pieces) – 1 pound

- Soy sauce – 5 tablespoons

- Salt – 2 teaspoons

- Pepper – 2 teaspoons

- Garlic (minced) – 1 clove

- Olive oil – 4 tablespoons

Instructions:

- Season the beef with salt and pepper.

- Heat the pan and add the cooking oil. When the oil is heated well, place the beef on the pan and cook for 5 minutes, then turn over the other side and continue to cook 5 minutes, too. Then remove the beef from the pan.

- Add 1 tablespoon of olive oil on the same pan, add the garlic, stir and add the soy sauce and ½ teaspoon of pepper, cook the sauce for 3 minutes.

- Pour the sauce of garlic and soy sauce into the cooked beef. Now it's ready to serve.

Chapter 2. Chicken

Being rich in nutrients and minerals, chicken is necessary food to many families, particularly women who are pregnant, chicken is the best source for protein, riboflavin, iron, vitamin B12 and Zinc that they should eat every day. One skinless chicken breast will give you about 54 g of protein and there will be 1.1 mg of Iron per 3 ounces of roast chicken. However, chicken is also high in cholesterol which can contribute to heart disease, so pregnant women should eat skinless chicken to be healthier. Here are the recipes can satisfy even the pickiest eaters.

1.Baked Garlic Chicken

Serving: 4

Total time: 30 minutes

Ingredients:

- Chicken breast – 3 pounds (48 ounces)

- Grated Parmesan cheese – 12 tablespoons

- Olive oil – 4 tablespoons

- Bread crumbs – 2/3 cup

- Chopped garlic – 5 cloves

- Garlic salt – ¼ teaspoon

Instructions:

- Preheat the oven to 425° F.

- Let olive oil be heated in a pan, then add garlic and garlic salt to blend the flavor.

- Mix the bread crumbs and grated parmesan cheese together in a bowl.

- Dip chicken breasts into the mixture of garlic and olive oil, then dip into the mixture of bread crumbs and grated parmesan cheese, put all in baking dish.

- Put the baking dish of chicken breasts in the oven and let it sit for 30 minutes, then serve.

2.Miso Honey Chicken

Serving: 4

Total time: 15 minutes

Ingredients:

- Chicken breasts – 4 pounds

- Honey – ½ cup

- White miso paste – ½ cup

- Sesame oil – 3 teaspoons

- Crushed red pepper – ½ teaspoon

Instructions:

- Preheat the grill to the medium heat.

- Add honey, sesame oil, miso pastes and crushed red pepper to a bowl, then mix them well together.

- Brush over the top of chicken breasts with mixture of honey and sesame oil.

- Grill the chicken breasts for 5 minutes for each side.

- They're ready to serve.

3.Pea Chicken Stir Fry

Serving: 2 - 3

Total time: 30 minutes

Ingredients:

- Boneless chicken breasts (cut into strips) – 3 pounds

- Green bean – 4 ounces

- Soy sauce – 1 tablespoon

- Lemon juice – 3 tablespoons

- Honey – 1 teaspoon

- Black pepper – 1 teaspoon

- Green onion and lemon zest for garnish (optional)

- Olive oil – 2 tablespoons

- Garlic (chopped) – 2 cloves

Instructions:

- Let olive oil heated in a pan over medium heat.

- Add garlic and cook for 2 minutes and add chicken to the pan, stir and cook for 5 minutes.

- Add green beans to the pan, soy sauce, honey and lemon juice, stir well and cook for 7 minutes or until the beans are tender, then add black pepper.

- Add green onion and adjust the season as desired and remove from heat.

- Serve with rice.

4.Bell Pepper and Chicken Stir Fry

Serving: 2 - 3

Total time: 30 minutes

Ingredients:

- Boneless Chicken (cut into bite-size pieces) – 8 ounces

- Bell pepper (cut into bite-size pieces) – 2 (1 red and 1 green)

- Onion (cut into thin slices) – 1 large

- Fish sauce – 2 tablespoons

- Oyster sauce – 1 tablespoon

- Sugar – 1 teaspoon

- Canola – 2 tablespoons

- Garlic (chopped) – 2 cloves

- Ginger (chopped) – 2 tablespoons

- Green onion (cut into 1-inch pieces) – 2

Instructions:

- Mix fish sauce, oyster sauce and sugar well together in a bowl.

- Heat the oil in a wok over high heat. Add garlic and cook for 1 minute, then add the chicken and ginger, stir and cook for 5 minutes.

- Add the bell pepper, green onions, onions, stir and cook for 3 minutes,

- Then add the mixture of sauce and cook for 3 minutes to let the chicken is cooked through and the bell peppers are crisp-tender.

- Remove the wok from heat. And your dish is ready to serve with rice.

5.10 Minute Thai Chicken Stir Fry

Serving: 2

Total time: 10 minutes

Ingredients:

- Boneless chicken (cut into ¾ inch pieces) – 1 pound

- Cooking oil – 2 tablespoons

- Garlic (chopped) – 2 cloves

- Onion (thin slices) – ½ cup

- Fish sauce – 2 tablespoons

- Sugar – 2 tablespoons

- Thai Chile – 1 or more (optional)

Instructions:

- Put oil in a wok and let it heated on medium heat. Add garlic and stir for 30 seconds, when the garlic gets fragrant then add chicken, cook and stir for 5 minutes.

- Add onion, fish sauce and Chile to the wok, and cook for 3 minutes more.

- When the chicken is cooked through, taste it to adjust the season as desired then remove the wok from heat.

- Then serve with rice.

6.Asian Pineapple Chicken Stir Fry

Serving: 4

Total time: 30 minutes

Ingredients:

- Chicken breast (skinless and boneless) – 1 pound

- Pineapple (cut into slices) – 1 cup

- Cornstarch – 2 tablespoons

- Ginger (chopped) – 1 teaspoon

- Cooking oil – 2 tablespoons

- Fish sauce – 1 tablespoon

- Garlic (minced) – 1 clove

- Thai Pineapple and chili sauce – ½ cup

Instructions:

- Mix cornstarch and fish sauce well together in a bowl, then place chicken in the mixture.

- Heat 1 tablespoon of oil in a skillet on medium high heat and add garlic and ginger, stir fry for 30 seconds, then add pineapple, stir and cook for 3 minutes.

- Add pineapple and Chile sauce, cook for 3 minutes more, then remove from skillet.

- Add 1 tablespoon of oil to the same skillet, let it heated, then add the chicken and stir fry until chicken is cooked through, often for 5 minutes.

- Add the cooked pineapple to the skillet, stir well together and cook until all are heated through, often 5 minutes more, then remove from heat, and it is better to pair with rice.

Chapter 3. Fish

People are often encouraged to take enough omega-3 fatty acids to reduce the risk of heart disease and eating fishes is considered one of the effective solutions for that. This is absolutely true because fishes are the best source for omega 3-fatty acids. How about the benefits of omega 3-fatty acids to pregnant women's health? Omega 3-fatty acids play a crucial role in the neurological and early visual development of the baby. Moreover, omega-3 fatty acids also impact the baby's intelligence after birth, as some studies showed, babies born to mothers who had high level of DHA (type of omega-3 fatty acids) in their blood will be smarter than others who had lower. However, eating fishes can be problematic for pregnant women if they don't have a right choice because some of fishes are very high in mercury which is bad for baby's development. Fatty fishes like salmon, sardine, tuna and trout are higher omega-3 fatty acids than others and bear in mind that four of these types including shark, swordfish, king mackerel and tilefish are very high in mercury. And now just add these healthy recipes for fish to your list as a way to meet your omega-3 fatty acid requirement.

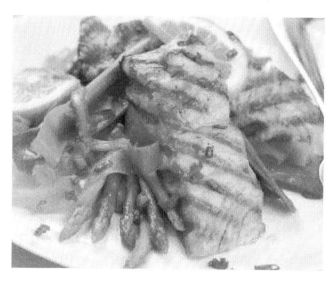

1.Sweet and Spicy Salmon

Serving: 2

Total time: 20 minutes

Ingredients:

- Boneless salmon fillet – 2 (1/2 lb. each)

- Cajun seasoning – 1 tablespoon

- Cooking oil – 2 teaspoons

- Brown sugar – 1 teaspoon

- Peach jam – 1 tablespoon

- Lemon juice – ½ teaspoon

Instructions:

- Mix sugar with Cajun seasoning well together in a bowl. Season the salmon fillets with the mixture of Cajun evenly.

- Heat oil in a non-stick pan over medium high heat, then place the salmon on the pan, cook for 5 minutes each side.

- Mix peach jam with lemon juice, then add this mixture to hot pan, let it coat evenly the fillets, cook until the sauce gets thicken.

- Remove fish from pan, you can eat salmon alone or pair it with any sauce.

2.Grilled Salmon with Foil

Serving: 2

Total time: 15 minutes

Ingredients:

- Boneless salmon fillet – 2 (3/4 inch thick each)

- Large piece of aluminum foil – 2

- White wine – ¼ cup

- Lemon (cut into thin slices) – 1

- Lemon juice – 3 tablespoons

- Olive oil – 3 tablespoons

- Kosher salt – ½ teaspoon

- Freshly ground black pepper – ½ teaspoon

- Caper – 1 tablespoon

Instructions:

- Heat your grill to 450 degrees.

- Place a piece of aluminum foil on a baking sheet, then place the salmon, skin side down on the baking sheet.

- Brush olive oil on top of salmon fillet and sprinkle with a bit salt and pepper, then white wine, lemon juice and capers, finally, place a slice of lemon on top.

- Place another piece of foil over the salmon, let salmon fillets wrapped tightly in foil.

- Place the salmon on grill and cook for 10 - 20 minutes, then take it out and serve.

3.Tomato Salmon

Serving: 2

Total time: 30 minutes

Ingredients:

- Salmon fillet – 2

- Grape tomato (cut into halve) – 1 cup

- Parchment paper – 2 (18-inche long pieces)

- Red onion (thin slices) – 4

- Basil leave – 5

- Olive oil – 1 tablespoon

- Balsamic vinegar – 1 tablespoon

- Salt – 1 teaspoon

- Pepper – 1 teaspoon

Instructions:

- Place a parchment paper on a baking sheet, spray with a bit cooking oil.

- Place salmon fillets on the baking sheet, then place grape tomatoes, onions and basil around the salmon and season all the ingredients with salt and pepper.

- Next is season all the ingredients with 1 tablespoon of olive oil and 1 tablespoon of Balsamic vinegar.

- Wrap salmon and veggies by folding it over itself, then bake the salmon at 400 degrees for 10 – 15 minutes.

- Remove from the oven, open and enjoy.

4.Salmon Stuffed Avocado

Serving: 4

Total time: 25 minutes

Ingredients:

- Smoked salmon (thin slices) – 5 ounces

- Avocado (halve) - 4

- Egg – 8

- Crushed red pepper flakes – ½ teaspoon

- Black pepper – 1 teaspoon

- Kosher salt – 2 teaspoons

- Baby spinach leave – 16

- Chopped chives – 2 teaspoons

Instructions:

- Preheat the oven to 425 degrees

- Halve the avocados, take out the seed. You can scoop out some flesh to get a larger hole.

- Place the slices of smoked salmon and spinach on the hole.

- Then crack an egg and place into the hole, season with a bit salt and pepper. Repeat the steps with the remaining avocados.

- Place the avocados on a baking sheet and bake in the oven for 15 – 20 minutes. Sprinkle with chives, red pepper flakes and serve.

5.Grilled Salmon with Mayonnaise Garlic Sauce

Serving: 4

Total time: 30 minutes

Ingredients:

- Salmon fillets – 4

- Mayonnaise – ½ cup

- Garlic (minced) – 4 cloves

- Olive oil – 2 tablespoons

- Dijon mustard – 2 tablespoons

- Fresh tarragon – 1 tablespoon

- Lemon juice – 1 tablespoon

- Finely grated lemon zest – 1 tablespoon

- Ground black pepper – ½ teaspoon

- Salt – 1 teaspoon

Instructions:

- Preheat the grill over high medium heat.

- Season the salmon with salt and pepper, and brush olive oil on salmon.

- Mix mayonnaise with olive oil, mustard, lemon juice, lemon zest, tarragon, salt and pepper in a bowl well together. Set aside.

- Lightly brush oil on the grill grate. Place salmon fillets on the grill and let them sit on the grill for 5 – 10 minutes.

- Place the cooked salmon on a dish and pour the sauce on top.

6.Salmon with Avocado Sauce

Serving: 4

Total time: 30 minutes

Ingredients:

- Salmon fillets – 4

- Avocado – 2

- Olive oil – 4 tablespoons

- Green onion (minced) – 1 tablespoon

- Parsley (minced) – 1 tablespoon

- Lime juice – 3 tablespoons

- Dijon mustard – 1 teaspoon

- Salt – 2 teaspoons

- Pepper – 1 teaspoon

Instructions:

- Add avocados, olive oil, green onions, parsley, lime juice, mustard, 1 teaspoon of salt and ½ teaspoon of pepper in a blender, press the button, then pour the mixture in a bowl.

- Season the salmon with a bit salt and pepper and sprinkle the pan with oil, heat it.

- Then place the salmon on the pan, skin side down, cook each side for 3 – 4 minutes to get the medium doneness.

- Remove from the pan, and serve with avocado sauce.

Chapter 4. Seafood

Women are encouraged to eat a variety of foods during pregnancy for the healthy development of baby. Seafood is also an essential food that pregnant women should not avoid because seafood types are packed with calcium, vitamin D, zinc and omega-3 fatty acids. For example, there will be 15 mg of zinc per 1 cup of oyster. Three ounces of canned sardine can give you about 35% of RDI for calcium and approximately 70% your daily needs for vitamin D. For such benefits of seafood to health, now it's time to enrich your healthy recipes to eat during pregnancy with these types of seafood.

1.Shrimp Avocado Salad

Serving: 2

Total time: 30 minutes

Ingredients:

- Shrimp – 2 pounds

- Avocado (cut into cubes) – 2

- Red onion (sliced) – 2 tablespoons

Dressing:

- Olive oil – ¼ cup

- Red wine vinegar – ¼ cup

- Garlic (minced) – ½ teaspoon

- Parsley (chopped) – 1 teaspoon

- Dijon mustard – 1 teaspoon

- Salt – 1 teaspoon

- Pepper – ½ teaspoon

Instructions:

- Add water and a bit salt to a large pot, bring to a boil over medium high heat, then add raw shrimp to the pot and cook for 10 – 15 minutes.

- Remove shrimp and put them to a bowl of cold water to cool quicker, then remove and let shrimps peeled and deveined.

- Place shrimps, avocado and onion in a bowl.

- Mix all the ingredients for dressing well together.

- Add the dressing to the bowl of shrimps and avocados. Now it's ready to serve.

2.Tuna Stuffed Avocado

Serving: 4

Total time: 15 minutes

Ingredients:

- Canned tuna – 2 cans (5-ounce each)

- Avocado (halved) – 4

- Mayonnaise – ¼ cup

- Celery (chopped) – ½ cup

- Sweet relish – 1 tablespoon

- Prepared yellow mustard – 1 teaspoon

- Lemon juice – 2 teaspoons

- Curry powder – ½ teaspoon

- Salt – 1 teaspoon

- Pepper – ½ teaspoon

Instructions:

- Halve the avocados, remove seeds.

- Mix tuna with celery, mayonnaise, sweet relish, mustard, lemon juice, curry powder, salt and pepper well together.

- Spoon the mixture of tuna into the hole of avocado and sprinkle a bit salt and pepper on top, repeat the same step until all avocados are completed, then enjoy.

3.Grilled Oyster

Serving: 4

Total time: 25 minutes

Ingredients:

- Oyster – 2 pounds

- Butter (softened) – 2 cups

- Finely grated Parmesan cheese – ½ cup

- Finely chopped parsley – ¼ cup

- Worcestershire sauce – 1 tablespoon

- Paprika – 1 teaspoon

- Ground red pepper – ½ teaspoon

- Hot sauce – ½ teaspoon

Instructions:

- Preheat the grill to 450 degrees.

- Add butter, parmesan cheese, parsley, Worcestershire sauce, paprika, ground red pepper, and hot sauce in a blender, mix them well together, then pour into a bowl.

- Arrange oysters on a grill, place a spoon of the mixture on each oyster, then grill for 7 minutes.

- When the edges of oyster's curl, remove, then serve.

4.Asparagus Shrimp Stir fry

Serving: 2

Total time: 20 minutes

Ingredients:

- Asparagus (cut into bite-size length) – 300g

- Shrimp (peeled and deveined) – 150 g

- Garlic (minced) – 3 cloves

- Soy sauce – 1 tablespoon

- Oyster sauce – 2 tablespoons

- Sugar – ½ teaspoon

- Ground white pepper – ¼ teaspoon

- Cooking oil – 2 tablespoons

- Water – ½ cup

Instructions:

- Mix sugar with soy sauce, oyster sauce in water, stir well.

- Heat oil in a wok, add garlic. When the garlic is fragrant, add shrimp, stir fry for 3 minutes then add asparagus. Continue to stir fry for 10 minutes,

- Add the mixture of sauce to the wok, cook and stir for 3 minutes more to get all ingredients cooked through.

- Take them out and place on a dish, then serve.

5.Grilled Sardine

Serving: 2

Total time: 20 minutes

Ingredients:

- Sardine – 1 pound

- Olive oil – 2 tablespoons

- Salt – ½ teaspoon

- Ground pepper – ¼ teaspoon

- Baguette (cut into thin slices) – 6 inch

- Garlic (minced) – 1 clove

- Lemon (wedged) – 1

Instructions:

- Preheat the grill over medium heat.

- Brush fishes evenly with oil, season them with salt and pepper.

- Brush cut bread with oil, season them salt and pepper and rub the garlic.

- Brush the grill with oil, place breads on the grill and cook until crisp, about 1 minute each side.

- Place sardines on grill and let them cooked 2 – 4 minutes each side, serve it with lemon wedges.

6.Tuna and White Bean Salad

Serving: 4

Total time: 10 minutes

Ingredients:

- White bean – 1 can (15 – 20 ounces each)

- Canned tuna – 1 can (6 ounces each)

- Lemon juice – 3 tablespoons

- Olive oil – 2 tablespoons

- Garlic (minced) – 1 clove

- Salt – 1 teaspoon

- Ground pepper – ½ teaspoon

- Red onion – ¼ cup

- Fresh parsley (chopped) – 3 tablespoons

- Fresh basil (chopped) - 3 tablespoons

Instructions:

- Mix lemon juice, oil, salt, pepper and garlic well together in a bowl.

- Add the remaining ingredients including onion, parsley, basil, bean and tuna.

- Mix them well, and serve.

Chapter 5. Bacon

You may be advisable to reduce consuming bacon or even completely avoid eating bacon during pregnancy because bacon often contains listeria and nitrites which can affect the healthy baby's development. But bacon still has benefits if you eat them the right ways, so what should you consider when you are craving for bacon? Eating bacon can be problematic if you eat uncooked bacon. However, it is completely safe for pregnant if you make sure that your bacon is reheated or cooked at least at 165 degrees. Moreover, to be healthier, you should choose the leaner types of bacon instead of fat bacon.

1.Easy Baked Bacon

Serving: 2

Total time: 20 minutes

Ingredients:

- Bacon (cut into thin long strips) – 1 pound

Instructions:

- Preheat the oven to 375 degrees F.

- Place the bacon strips on the baking sheet and put it in the oven and let it sit for 15 – 20 minutes.

- Remove from the oven and place them on a paper to drain.

- Serve.

2.Bacon Spinach and Bacon Dressing

Serving: 2

Total time: 30 minutes

Ingredients:

- Bacon (thin strips) – 1 pound

- Baby spinach – 2 cups

- Sugar – 1 tablespoon

- Dijon mustard – 2 heaping teaspoons

- Red wine vinegar – 3 tablespoons

- Red onion (thin slices) – 3 and 1 teaspoon of chopped onion

- Mushroom (slices) – 4 large

- Garlic (minced) – 1 clove

- Salt – 1 teaspoon

- Pepper – ½ teaspoon

- Cooking oil – 2 tablespoons

Instructions:

- Heat the oil in a pan over medium high heat, then add the bacon and fry for 5 – 10 minutes. Remove bacon and use a sieve to drain and get the warm oil.

- In the same pan, heat a bit of oil, and add chopped onions, garlic until they are brown and fragrant. Add vinegar, ¼ cup of water, 1 tablespoon of sugar, then 2 teaspoons of Dijon mustard, 1 teaspoon of salt and ½ teaspoon of pepper whisk them well together,

- Then mix 1 tablespoon of cornstarch with 1 tablespoon of water, add this mixture to the pan, stir well until the sauce is thicken, then add the fat and cooked bacon, too. Taste it and adjust the season as desired.

- Combine baby spinach, mushrooms, red onions in a bowl, then pour the warm bacon dressing, and mix them well.

- It's ready to serve.

Note: You can also regulate the ingredients by adding tomato slices and hard cooked eggs in the salad if you like.

3.Spiced Bacon

Serving: 2

Total time: 30 minutes

Ingredients:

- Bacon (cut into strips) – 1 pound

- Ground mustard – 1 teaspoon

- Ground cinnamon – ¼ teaspoon

- Ground nutmeg – ¼ teaspoon

- Dash cayenne pepper –

- Brown sugar – ¼ cup

Instructions:

- Preheat the oven to 350 degrees F.

- Combine sugar, mustard, cinnamon, nutmeg and cayenne pepper together.

- Rub the bacon strips with the mixture of mustard.

- Let the bacon strips for 20 – 25 minutes.

- It's ready to serve.

4.Cinnamon Bacon

Serving: 2

Total time: 10 minutes

Ingredients:

- Bacon (cut into strips) – 1 pound

- Ground cinnamon – ½ cup

- White sugar – ½ cup

Instructions:

- Preheat your skillet over medium heat.

- Add cinnamon and sugar in a bowl and mix them well together.

- Rub the mixture of cinnamon and sugar on the bacon strips, then place them on the hot skillet and cook for 10 minutes.

- Remove and serve.

5.Fried Bacon with Paprika

Serving: 2

Total time: 15 minutes

Ingredients:

- Bacon (cut into thin strips) – 1 pound

- Paprika – 1 tablespoon

- Granulated garlic – 1 tablespoon

- Water – 1/3 cup

Instructions:

- Add garlic, paprika and water in a bowl, stir well together.

- Heat the skillet over medium high, and add the mixture and bacon strips to the skillet, cook for 10 minutes until the bacon coated with paprika and garlic, then reduce the heat.

- It's ready.

6.Easy Baked Bacon with Paprika

Serving: 2

Total time: 15 minutes

Ingredients:

- Bacon strips – 1 pound

- Paprika – 1 tablespoon

- Sugar – 1/2 tablespoon

Instructions:

- Mix paprika and sugar well together.

- Rub the mixture on both sides of bacon strips.

- Place the bacon strips to the baking sheet at 350 degrees for 15 – 17 minutes.

- Remove and serve.

Chapter 6. Pork

During pregnancy, the protein need is higher than normal to support the fetal growth and the placenta's growth and a pregnant woman is recommended to take from 76 – 100 g of protein per day. Therefore, with 3-ounce serving of pork, you are given about one-third of your daily needs of protein.

1.Garlic Lime Marinated Pork Chop

Serving: 4

Total time: 30 minutes

Ingredients:

- Lean pork chop – 4 (6 ounces each)

- Garlic (minced) – 4 cloves

- Cumin – ½ teaspoon

- Chili powder – ½ teaspoon

- Paprika – ½ teaspoon

- Lime juice – ½ teaspoon

- Lime zest – 1 teaspoon

- Salt – 1 teaspoon

- Pepper – 1 teaspoon

Instructions:

- Add garlic, paprika, chili powder, cumin, salt and pepper to a bowl, then mix them well together.

- Add lime juice and lime zest, stir and add pork chops to the bowl to marinate for 20 minutes.

- Grill the pork chops for 4 – 5 minutes each side.

- It's done.

2.Grilled Pork Chops with Rosemary

Serving: 4

Total: 30 minutes

Ingredients:

- Lean pork chops – 4 (6 ounces each)

- Garlic (minced) – 4 cloves

- Olive oil – 1 teaspoon

- Lemon juice – ¼ cup

- Rosemary leave – 1 teaspoon

- Salt – 1 teaspoon

- Ground pepper – ½ teaspoon

Instructions:

- Mix olive oil with lemon juice, rosemary and garlic well together in a bowl.

- Season the pork chops with salt and pepper, then let them marinate in a mixture for 20 minutes.

- Then, grill pork chops for 10 minutes for both sides.

- Serve.

3.Pork Stir Fry with Onion

Serving: 4

Total time: 20 minutes.

Ingredients:

- Boneless pork chops (slices) – 1 pound

- Soy sauce – 1 tablespoon

- Cornstarch – 1 teaspoon

- Peanut oil/canola – 4 tablespoons

- Sesame oil – ½ teaspoon

- Garlic (minced) – 5 cloves

- Green onion (cut into 2 inch pieces) – 10

Instructions:

- Mix soy sauce, sugar and cornstarch well together in a bowl, add slices to the bowl for marinade for 10 minutes.

- Heat the peanut oil in a wok, then add the garlic and stir fry for 30 seconds for getting fragrant, then add slices of pork to the wok, stir fry for 3 minutes.

- Add the sesame oil and green onions and continue to stir fry for 3 minutes. When all ingredients are cooked through. Turn off the heat

- Place pork green onion stir fry on the dish and serve with rice.

4.Pork Stir Fry with Ginger and Honey

Serving: 2

Total time: 20 minutes

Ingredients:

- Pork (cut into bite-size pieces) – 250g

- Egg noodle – 2

- Corn flour – 2 teaspoons

- Soy sauce – 2 tablespoons

- Honey – 1 tablespoon

- Sunflower oil – 1 tablespoon

- Garlic (chopped) – 2 cloves

- Green pepper (sliced) – 1

- Mange tout – 100g

- Sesame seed – 1 teaspoon

Instructions:

- Boil water in a pot with a bit salt and cook the noodle for 2 minutes and drain, divide it into two bowls.

- Meanwhile, mix corn flour with 1 tablespoon of water, and add soy sauce and honey, stir all well together. Set aside.

- Heat the oil in a wok add pork, ginger, garlic, pepper and mange tout, stir fry and cook for 5 minutes.

- Add the mixture of corn flour, soy sauce and honey to the wok, stir and cook until the sauce bubbles.

- Pour the cooked pork on top of noodle with a bit sesame seeds and serve.

5.Pork Chop with Pear Sauce

Serving: 4

Total time: 30 minutes

Ingredients:

- Pork chops – 4

- Pear (diced) – 1

- Chicken stock – 1½ cup

- Vinegar – 3 tablespoons

- Honey – 2 tablespoons

- Ginger – 2 tablespoons

- Shallot (minced) – 1/3 cup

- Unsalted butter – 2 tablespoons

- Canola – 2 tablespoons

- Rosemary (minced) – ½ teaspoon

- Ground black pepper – ½ teaspoon

- Salt – 1 teaspoon

Instructions:

- Season the pork with a bit of salt.

- Heat the pan over medium high heat, place the pork chops on the pan for 5 – 10 minutes each side then remove them from the pan.

- In the same pan, add 1 tablespoon oil to the pan, heat and add ginger, shallots and butter, stir well to combine and cook for 1 minute.

- Add diced pear to the pan, stir for 3 minutes then add chicken stock, vinegar, and honey. Bring to boil for 5 minutes.

- Add rosemary, black pepper and salt then remove from heat. Serve this sauce with pork.

6. Fried Pork with Japanese Style

Serving: 2

Total time: 20 minutes

Ingredients:

- Pork (thin slices) – ¼ pound

- Miso – 1 tablespoon

- Mirin – tablespoon

- Gochujang / sweet hot sauce – 2 teaspoons

- Ginger (minced) – 1 teaspoon

- Garlic (minced) – 1 clove

Instructions:

- Mix the ingredients including ginger, gochujang, miso and mirin well together in a bowl.

- Coat slices of pork evenly with the mixture.

- Heat the pan, and add a little oil, then add the pork to the pan, cook until the pork slices are brown.

- Then serve with rice.

Chapter 7. Egg

Although cholesterol found high in eggs is often believed as a negative word, it actually plays an important role in the body. Not only is a structural molecule which is an important part of every single cell membrane but also makes steroid hormones like estrogen, cortisol and testosterone. Also, the truth is our liver has to produce cholesterol for the body's using if we can't get enough cholesterol from food. Therefore, instead of skipping this nutrient-rich food, you should know these facts. First, there are about 186 mg of cholesterol contained in each egg. Second, a healthy individual is recommended to consume 300 mg of cholesterol per day. Hence, the total egg you should eat for a day is about 2 eggs. However, the cholesterol doesn't come solely in eggs, the other foods you consume every day also contain cholesterol, therefore, as my personally final recommendation, you should eat about 3 eggs per week.

1.Scrambled Egg and Avocado

Serving: 2

Total time: 10 minutes

Ingredients:

- Egg – 2

- Milk – 1 tablespoon

- Butter – 1 teaspoon

- Avocado (diced) – 1

- Chives (chopped) – 1 teaspoon

Instructions:

- Mix the egg with milk in a bowl, whisk them well for 1 minute.

- Heat the skillet, add the butter to the skillet.

- Add the mixture of egg and milk, stir occasionally.

- Add the avocado, and stir.

- Top with chopped chives and serve with your sandwich.

2.Baked Avocado on Egg

Serving: 2

Total time: 17 minutes

Ingredients:

- Egg – 1

- Avocado (halved) – 1

- Pepper jack cheese – 2 ounces

- Salt – ½ teaspoon

- Pepper – ¼ spoon

Instructions:

- Preheat your oven to 425 degrees.

- Crack eggs and place into hole of avocado, then season the egg with salt and pepper.

- Bake the avocado in the oven for 15 minutes.

- Remove and serve.

3.Baked Egg with Mozzarella Cheese

Serving: 2

Total time: 20 minutes

Ingredients:

- Egg – 2

- Mozzarella cheese – ¼ cup

- Ea. tater tots (cooked and crumbled) – 12

- Butter – 1 teaspoon

- Jalapeno (diced) – 1 tablespoon

- Garlic (minced) – 1 clove

- Onion – ¼ cup

- Salt – ½ teaspoon

- Pepper – ¼ teaspoon

Instructions:

- Preheat the oven to 350 degrees.

- Add the butter to a hot skillet and let it melt, then add onion and jalapeno stir and cook for 2 minutes, then add the garlic and cook 1 minute more.

- Divide the crumbled tots into two portions, then place on two ramekin dishes. Add the mixture of onion and garlic to the dishes, add mozzarella on the top.

- Put an egg on each ramekin, season the eggs with salt and pepper, then bake for 5 minutes.

- Remove from the oven and serve.

4.Easy Egg and Bacon

Serving: 4

Total time: 20 minutes

Ingredients:

- Egg (hard boiled) – 10

- Bacon (cooked and crumbled) – 4 strips

- Cream cheese (softened) – 4 ounces

- Mayonnaise – 2 tablespoons

- Dijon mustard – 2 teaspoons

- Chive (chopped) – 3 tablespoons

Instructions:

- Halve all eggs and remove the yolks.

- Mix cream cheese and mayonnaise well together, until the mixture is fluffy, then add egg yolks, mustard, salt and pepper, mix well all the ingredients together.

- Mix bacon and chopped chives and stir.

- Spoon the mixture of egg yolk on the white eggs, and top with bacon and chives.

- Serve.

5.Tomato Baked Egg

Serving: 3

Total: 30 minutes

Ingredients:

- Egg – 6

- Tomato (sliced) – 2

- Onion (diced) – ½

- Garlic (minced) – 1 clove

- Grated Monterrey jack cheese – ½ cup

- Butter – 2 tablespoons

- Cilantro (chopped) – 3 teaspoons

- Salt – 1 teaspoon

- Pepper – ½ teaspoon

Instructions:

- Preheat the oven to 350 degrees F.

- Heat the skillet and melt the butter. Let the butter spread on the bottom evenly.

- Add the garlic, onion and tomato to the skillet then top with grated cheese.

- Crack all egg and place on the skillet.

- Bake for 20 minutes then remove from the oven. Place cilantro on top and sprinkle a little salt and pepper. Serve.

6.A Perfect Omelet

Serving: 2

Total time: 15 minutes

Ingredients:

- Egg – 2

- Butter – 1 teaspoon

- Pepper – ¼ teaspoon

- Water – 2 tablespoons

- Shredded cheese – 1/3 cup

- Baby spinach – ½ cup

Instructions:

- Mix eggs and water together, whisk them well in a bowl.

- Heat the non-stick pan and melt the butter on the pan. Let the butter coat evenly to the bottom of the pan.

- Pour the mixture of egg to the pan, cook for 5 - 10 minutes then carefully turn the other side of egg with a spatula to have your egg cooked through.

- Place baby spinach and chopped ham on top, then fold omelet in half. Serve.

Chapter 8. Pasta

During pregnancy women often become picky eaters, especially in the first trimester of pregnancy while morning sickness is occurring, they often just crave for some certain food and sometimes have an aversion to certain foods. But try these delicious recipes for pasta, the special taste of the combination of pasta and avocado or tomato sauce may help you find your good appetite again, most importantly these recipes can give you not only a lot of nutrients but also energy for a whole day of working.

1.Penne Pasta and Mushroom with Feta Cheese

Serving: 4

Total time: 30 minutes

Ingredients:

- Pasta – 6 ounces
- Mushroom – ½ pound
- Crumbled Feta cheese – 1/3 cup
- Olive oil – 1 tablespoon
- Tomato – 1 can (14 ½ ounces)
- Salt – ¼ teaspoon
- Basil (dried) – 1 teaspoon

Instructions:

- Add water to a pot, bring to boil and add pasta to cook. When it is ready, remove and drain.
- Meanwhile, heat oil in a pan and stir fry mushroom for 5 minutes.
- Add tomato, salt and basil, cook and stir for 5 minutes.
- Add the cooked pasta, and cheese, stir to mix them well.
- Serve.

2.Avocado Pasta

Serving: 1 - 2

Total time: 30 minutes.

Ingredients:

- Pasta – 200 grams

- Avocado – 1 large

- Lemon juice – 1 tablespoon

- Garlic (minced) – 1 clove

- Greek yogurt – 2 tablespoons

- Honey – 1 teaspoon

- Basil (dried) – 1 teaspoon

- Onion (diced) – ½

- Grape tomato (halved) – ¼ cup

- Salt – ½ teaspoon

- Pepper – ¼ teaspoon

Instructions:

- In a large pot, add water, bring to boil and cook pasta.

- Meanwhile, mix smashed avocado with yogurt, honey, lemon juice, garlic and basil, salt and pepper together in a bowl.

- When the pasta is ready, remove and drain, then add to the mixture of avocado, then add red onion, grape tomatoes.

- Serve.

3.Broccoli Pasta

Serving: 3 - 4

Total time: 30 minutes

Ingredients:

- Pasta – 1 pound

- Broccoli – 2 cups

- Chicken (drained and flaked) – 1 can (6 ounces)

- Olive oil – 3 tablespoons

- Garlic (minced) – 4 cloves

- Parsley (chopped) – ¾ cup

- Red pepper flakes – ½ teaspoon

- Salt – ½ teaspoon

- Ground black pepper – ½ teaspoon

Instructions:

- In a large pot, add water, bring to boil and add pasta and cook, when the pasta is done, add broccoli to the pot you've cooked pasta. Drain pasta and broccoli.

- Meanwhile, heat the pan, add the oil to the pan. When oil is heated, add garlic and pepper flakes for 1 minute.

- Add the chicken, ½ cup of reserved pasta cooking water, parsley, salt and pepper cook for 2 minutes.

- Add the mixture of chicken to pasta, broccoli, and the remaining ½ cup pasta cooking water. Heat all the ingredients through for 5 minutes.

- Serve.

4.Tomato Sauce Pasta

Serving: 2

Total time: 20 minutes

Ingredients:

- Pasta – 500 grams

- Tomato sauce – 1 cup

- Olive oil –

- Onion (chopped) – 1

- Parsley – 1 teaspoon

- Garlic (minced) – 1 clove

- Chili flake – ½ teaspoon

- Black pepper – ¼ teaspoon

- Salt – 1 teaspoon

Instructions:

- Cook pasta according to the instructions on the package, then remove and drain when it's done.

- Heat the pan and add the oil. When the oil is heated, add garlic to the pan, stir fry for 30 seconds, then add onions and continue to cook for 1 minute or until both onion and garlic are light brown.

- Add tomato sauce, stir and add 1 teaspoon of salt, chili flakes, and black pepper cook for 3 minutes.

- Then add your pasta to the pan, stir to mix pasta with sauce well, cook for another 3 minutes to heat through and add the parsley to the pan.

- You can also add cheese to the pasta, and then serve.

5.Sweet Peas and Nutshell Pasta

Serving: 4

Total time: 30 minutes

Ingredients:

- Nutshell pasta – 4 cups

- Frozen pea (thawed) – 1 ½ cup

- Stalk celery (chopped) – 1

- Red onion (chopped) – ½

- Fresh parsley (chopped) – ½ cup

- Can tuna – 2 (6 ounces each)

- Olive oil – 1/3 cup

- Red wine vinegar – ¼ cup

- Dijon – ½

- Kosher salt and black pepper

Instructions:

- Add water to the pot, cook it.

- Mix pasta, tuna, peas, onion, parsley and celery well together.

- For the dressing, mix oil, vinegar, mustard well together, then season with 1 teaspoon of salt and ¼ teaspoon pepper in a bowl.

- Dress the mixture of pasta and gently toss to combine.

- Serve

6.Parmesan Chicken Pasta

Serving: 4

Total time: 30 minutes

Ingredients:

- Pasta – 12 ounces

- Rotisserie chicken – 2 pounds

- Fresh rosemary (chopped) – 2 tablespoons

- Kosher salt and pepper

Instructions:

- Cook pasta in a large pot as instructions on the package. When the pasta is done, reserve 1 ¼ cups of cooking water, drain the pasta.

- Meanwhile, shred the chicken and remove the skin and bones.

- Combine the pasta with chicken, rosemary, reserved pasta water, ½ cup of parmesan cheese, salt (1/2 teaspoon) and bit pepper in a bowl, mix them well.

- Cook and stir until the sauce is thicken, and add the remaining Parmesan.

- Serve.

Chapter 9. Noodle

And now is a collection of very yummy recipes for noodle that come from Asia and somewhere else. Although some of them are quite long list of ingredients, they won't take you too much time to prepare and completed.

1.Vietnamese Rice Noodle

Serving: 4

Total time: 30 minutes

Ingredients:

- Dried rice noodle – 12 ounces

- Cabbage leaves – 4

- Carrot (julienned) – 2

- Cucumber (thinly small and long slices) – 1

- Cilantro (chopped) – 1 cup

- Fish sauce – 3 tablespoons

- Garlic (minced) – 5 cloves

- Jalapeno pepper – ½ teaspoon

- Lime juice – ¼ cup

- Sugar – 3 tablespoons

- Unsalted peanut – ¼ cup

- Fresh mint (chopped) – 4 sprigs

Instructions:

- In a bowl, mix garlic, fish sauce, sugar, lime juice, cilantro and pepper together, stir well. Set aside.

- Add water and a bit of salt to a pot, bring to a boil then cook dried noodle for 3 minutes. Remove the noodle and place it to a container of cold water then drain it well. Let it cool.

- Pour mixture of fish sauce to the noodle, add carrot, cucumber and cabbage, mix them well. Top with peanuts and mint.

- Serve.

2.Chicken Noodle and Ginger Sauce

Serving: 6

Total time: 30 minutes

Ingredients:

- Cooked chicken – 3 cups

- Rice noodle – 6 ounces

- Carrot (cut into matchstick) – 2

- Red pepper (cut into small and long slices) – 1

- Roasted peanut (chopped) – ½ cup

- Water – 8 cups

- Vinegar – 2 tablespoons

For the sauce

- Peanut butter – ½ cup

- Lime juice – 4 ½ tablespoons

- Soy sauce – 3 tablespoons

- Honey – 3 tablespoons

- Ginger (chopped) – 2 tablespoons

- Sesame oil – 1 ½ teaspoons

- Vinegar – 3 tablespoons

- Kosher salt – ¼ teaspoon

- Crushed chili – ¼ teaspoon

Instructions:

- Add all the sauce ingredients to a blender, press the button, then mix them well.

- Boil water in a pot, when it is boiled, often for 10 – 15 minutes, add vinegar and a bit of salt to the pot, add dried noodle and cook for 3 minutes.

- Place noodle in a cold water, drain it well.

- Pour the sauce into the noodle, add carrots and red pepper, mix them well, top with the peanuts.

- Serve.

3.Beef Noodle Stir Fry

Serving: 2

Total time: 25 minutes

Ingredients:

- Beef (thin slices) – 1 pound

- Noodle – 2 packages

- Carrot (thin slices) – 1

- Red pepper (thin slices) – 1

- Broccoli (cooked and cut into small pieces) – 1 floret

- Fish sauce – 3 tablespoons

- Garlic (minced) – 1 clove

- Onion (chopped) - 1

- Salt – ½ teaspoon

- Pepper – ¼ teaspoon

Instructions:

- Add the water to a pot, bring to a boil, add the noodle to the pot and cook for 1 minute, remove and drain.

- With the remaining water, cook the broccoli for 3 minutes.

- After that, heat the oil in a pan, add the minced garlic, chopped onion and stir for 30 seconds until fragrant.

- Then add the beef to the pan stir for 3 minutes, then add broccoli, carrot, red pepper and fish sauce, salt and pepper, stir and cook for another 5 minutes to make sure all ingredients are tender.

- Serve.

4.Chinese Noodle

Serving: 4

Total time: 30 minutes

Ingredients:

- Chow Mein noodles (or any kind of instant noodle) – 1 package (227g)

- Stock chicken – ½ cup

- Oyster sauce – 1/3 cup

- Cauliflower (cut into smaller pieces) – ½ of big floret

- Baby corn – 125 g

- Ground white pepper – ½ teaspoon

- Corn flour – 1 teaspoon

- Onion (thin slices) – 2

- Oil – 2 tablespoons

- Garlic (chopped) – 2 cloves

- Ginger (chopped) – 1 pieces of 2cm piece

Instructions:

- Heat the oil in a wok, add garlic, onion and ginger to the wok, stir fry for 1 minute and add cauliflower and baby corn, continue to cook for 3 minutes.

- Add oyster sauce and pepper, stir fry for 2 minutes.

- Mix corn flour with chicken stock together in a bowl. Add this mixture to the wok, stir to mix it well with vegetable.

- When the mixture begins to thicken, add noodle and stir for 3 minute.

- Remove the wok and place the noodle on a plate.

5.Very Simple Stir Fry Noodle

Serving: 4

Total time: 30 minutes

Ingredients:

- Steam fried Chinese noodle – 7 ounces

- Ginger – 6 slices

- Green onion (cut into 1-inch strips) – 2

- Oil – 3 tablespoons

For the sauce:

- Oyster sauce – 3 tablespoons

- Soya sauce – 2 tablespoons

- Sesame oil – 1 tablespoon

Instructions:

- Add water to a pot, bring to a boil, cook noodle for 2 minutes, remove and drain.

- Add oil to a pan. When it is heated, add ginger, and onion to the pan, stir fry until fragrant.

- Add noodle, stir fry for 5 minutes.

- Add the mixture of sauce, toss to coat.

- Serve.

6.Noodle Stir Fry with Shrimp

Serving: 6

Total time: 30 minutes

Ingredients:

- Noodle (linguini) – 12 ounces

- Shrimp (peeled and deveined with tails removed) – 2 pounds

- Soy sauce – ½ cup

- Cornstarch – 8 teaspoons

- Fresh ginger (grated) – ½ tablespoon

- Garlic (minced) – 6 cloves

- Sesame oil – 4 teaspoons

- Carrot (shredded) – 2 cups

- Cabbage (thin slices) – 2 cups

- Chicken broth – ½ cup

- Green onion (cut into strips) – 7

Instructions:

- Let shrimp marinated in the mixture of soy sauce, garlic, ginger and cornstarch for 10 minutes.

- Meanwhile, cook the noodle in a large pot for 1 minute. (10 minutes to wait for water being boiled and 1 minutes to cook the noodle).

- Remove shrimp, and drain. Heat 2 teaspoons of sesame oil in a wok, add the shrimp and stir fry for 3 minutes. When the shrimps are pink, it is alright to remove from the wok.

- Add the remaining sesame oil to the same wok, then add carrot, cabbage and stir fry for 2 minutes. Pour the chicken broth and the reserve marinade to the wok.

- When the mixture of carrot, cabbage and chicken broth is cooked through, return the cooked shrimps to the wok and cook.

- Pour the mixture of cooked shrimps in chicken broth to the cooked noodle. Mix them well, top with green onions and serve.

Chapter 10. Salads

All fruits and any kinds of vegetables are always good for health due to being high in fiber, vitamins and nutrients. Especially when you are pregnant, you are encouraged to eat more fruits and vegetables for enough fiber intake in order to prevent you from constipation and lower risk of cholesterol level. Therefore, there is no other source for fiber better than a bowl of colorful fruit salads or crunchy green salad, so let's give a try for each of these salad recipes.

1.Avocado and Mango Salad

Serving: 2

Total time: 25 minutes

Ingredients:

- Avocado (bite-size pieces) – 1

- Mango (bite-size pieces) – 1

- Baby spinach – 2 cups

- Unsweetened coconut – 4 tablespoons

For the dressing:

- Dijon mustard – 2 teaspoons

- Mayonnaise – 1 tablespoon

- Honey – 1 tablespoon

- Avocado oil – ¾ cup

- Lime juice – 3 tablespoons

- Orange juice – 3 tablespoons

- Lemon juice – 3 tablespoons

- Shallot (minced) – 1 tablespoon

- Poppy seed – 1 tablespoon

- Salt and pepper.

Instructions:

- Combine all the ingredients including mustard, mayonnaise, honey, shallot, lemon juice, lime juice and orange juice in a bowl, mix them well together. Then add oil, poppy seeds, salt and pepper and whisk well. This mixture will be used for dressing the salad.

- Combine baby spinach, mango, avocado and unsweetened coconut in a bowl, then dressing the mixture of mustard and mayonnaise to the salad, gently mix them well.

- Serve.

2.Chicken Grape Salad

Serving: 3

Total time: 30 minutes

Ingredients:

- Chicken (cooked and cut into ½ inch pieces) – 1 pound

- Grape (halved) – 1 cup

- Dried cherry – ½ cup

- Roasted pecan (chopped) – ½ cup

- Mayonnaise – 1 cup

- Celery (chopped) – 1 cup

- Salt – ½ teaspoon

- Black pepper – ¼ teaspoon

Instructions:

- In a bowl, combine chicken, grape, dried cherries, roasted pecan mayonnaise, celery together, season salad with salt and pepper, mix them well.

- It's done.

3.Strawberry Salad

Serving: 2

Total time: 10 minutes

Ingredients:

- Strawberry (halved) – 1 cup

- Red pepper (cut into bite-size pieces) – ½ cup

- Sweet onion (diced) – 1/3 cup

- Avocado (cut into bite-size pieces) – 1

- Jalapeno – 1

- Cilantro – ¼ cup

- Lemon juice – 1

- Salt – ½ teaspoon

Instructions:

- Combine all the ingredients together in a bowl.

- Put in the refrigerator for at least 20 minutes.

- Serve.

4.Simple Tomato Salad

Serving: 1

Total time: 10

Ingredients:

- Grape tomato (halved) – 1 cup

- Feta cheese – ¼ cup

- Balsamic vinegar – 2 tablespoons

- Olive oil – 1 tablespoon

- Salt – ½ teaspoon

- Pepper – ¼ teaspoon

Instructions:

- Mix all the ingredients together.

- Serve.

5.Quick Green Salad

Serving: 2

Total time: 10 minutes

Ingredients:

- Green salad (torn) – a bowl

- Dijon mustard – 1 teaspoon

- Mayonnaise – 2 teaspoons

- Champagne vinegar – 1 tablespoon

- Sugar – 1 teaspoon

- Salt – ½ teaspoon

- Pepper – ¼ teaspoon

Instructions:

- Combine Dijon mustard, mayonnaise, champagne vinegar, sugar, salt and pepper in a bowl, whisk them well until the mixture is smooth.

- Dress the salad green with this mixture.

- Serve.

6.Dried Cherry and Romaine Lettuce Salad

Serving: 3 - 4

Total time: 15 minutes

Ingredients:

- Romaine lettuce (torn) – 6 cups

- Dried cherry – ¼ cup

- Olive oil – 2 tablespoons

- Dijon mustard – 1 teaspoon

- Crumbled Feta cheese – 2 tablespoons

- Balsamic vinegar - 3 tablespoons

- Shallot (minced) – 1 tablespoon

- Fresh parsley (chopped) – 1 tablespoon

- Garlic (minced) – 1 clove

- Salt – 1 teaspoon

- Black pepper – ¼ teaspoon

Instructions:

- In a bowl, combine Dijon mustard, olive oil, shallot, garlic, parsley, balsamic vinegar together, then season the mixture a little salt and pepper, whisk them well.

- Dressing the mixture to the combination of lettuce and dried cherries, then top with crumble feta cheese.

- Serve.

Chapter 11. Snacks

Are you looking for something to eat in the late afternoon when your lunch has gone away for several hours but the dinner is still several hours left to come? With these simple and quick snack recipes, I bet that they will make you mouth-watering.

1.Chocolate Almond

Serving: 4

Total time: 15 minutes.

Ingredients:

- Almond – 1 cup

- Chocolate – 6 ounces

- Sugar and salt.

Instructions:

- Place a parchment paper on a baking sheet.

- Let the chocolate melted in a heat-proof bowl in a microwave for 30 seconds.

- Add all the almonds to the bowl of chocolate, be sure that all almonds are coated with chocolate.

- Take the almonds out of the bowl of chocolate, then place on the baking sheet.

- Season the almonds with a little sugar and salt, the put the baking sheet in the refrigerator.

Note:

You can bake the almonds at 300°F for about 10 minutes before coating with chocolate to get the extra flavor.

2.Chocolate Covered Strawberry

Serving: 4

Total time: 4

Ingredients:

- Strawberry – 1 pint

- Chocolate – 1 cup

- Coconut oil – 2 teaspoons

Instructions:

- Place a parchment paper on a baking sheet.

- Melt the chocolate and coconut oil in a heat-proof bowl in a microwave for 2 minutes.

- Dip the strawberries in the chocolate liquid, then place them on the baking sheet lined with parchment paper.

- Put the baking sheet in the fridge for 15 minutes to set.

- Keep the chocolate coated strawberries in the fridge for up 3 days.

3.Glazed Cashews

Serving: 2

Total time: 30 minutes

Ingredients:

- Cashew – 2 cups

- Sugar – ½ cup

- Chili sauce – ½ cup

- Ponzi sauce – 2 tablespoons

- Sesame seed – 3 tablespoons

- Dried pineapple – ½ cup

Instructions:

- Preheat the oven to 300 degrees.

- Combine all the ingredients, bring to a boil, and let it bubble for 1 minute.

- Reduce the heat, and let it simmer. When the liquid almost disappears, turn off the heat.

- Place the mixture of cashews on a baking sheet lined with a parchment paper, then place the baking sheet in the oven, bake for 20 minutes.

- Remove and let cool down. You can store it in an air tight container.

4.Sweet Potato Chips

Serving: 4

Total time: 30 minutes

Ingredients:

- Sweet potato (cut into thin slices) – 2 pounds

- Olive oil – 4 tablespoons

- Salt – 1 teaspoon

Instructions:

- Place the slices of sweet potato in a bowl. Add olive oil, then toss to coat evenly both sides of slices.

- Place the slices of sweet potato on a baking sheet lined with a parchment paper.

- Sprinkle a bit salt on top of slices.

- Put in the oven and bake at 425 degrees for 10 minutes.

- Remove, cool down and keep them in an air-tight container.

5.Fried Avocado with Egg and Panko

Serving: 2

Total time: 30 minutes.

Ingredients:

- Avocado (cut into wedges) – 2

- Flour – ½ cup

- Egg (whisked) – 1

- Panko – ½ cup

Sauce ingredients:

- Greek yogurt – ¼ cup

- Mayonnaise – 3 tablespoons

- Lemon juice – 1 tablespoon

- Paprika – ½ teaspoon

- Garlic (minced) – 1 clove

- Parsley (chopped) – 3 teaspoons

- Olive oil – 1 tablespoon

Ingredients:

- Preheat the oven to 450 degrees.

- Place egg, flour and panko in three separate bowls, then add a little salt and pepper in the bowl of flour and mix them well.

- For the sauce, mix all the sauce ingredients together in a bowl, season with a little salt and pepper, too.

- Dip the wedges of avocado in flour, egg and panko, then place on a baking sheet.

- Put the baking sheet in the oven and bake for 20 minutes, then remove, serve with the sauce.

6.Cherry Pie Bars

Serving: 4

Total time: 20 minutes

Ingredients:

- Raw almond – 1 ½ cups

- Dried cherry – 1 ½ cups

- Medjool date – 10

- Water

Instructions:

- Add all the ingredients in a blender, press the button until all ingredients are mixed well together.

- Place a parchment paper on a baking dish.

- Press the mixture of almond on the baking dish.

- Put in the refrigerator until it is firmed up.

- Cut it into small square bars.

Chapter 12. Dessert

The main purpose for having desert after main dishes is to aid your digestion, especially containing probiotics, yogurt can promote both of your digestive and immune system, why it is intentionally used as being central ingredient for most of these desert recipes.

1.Yogurt and Banana Parfait

Serving: 1

Total time: 5 minutes

Ingredients:

- Plain low-fat yogurt – ½ cup

- Banana (sliced) – ½

- Apple butter – 3 tablespoons

Instructions:

- Add yogurt in a glass, then slices of banana and top with apple butter.

- Serve.

Note. You can also add a little of cinnamon if

you like.

2.Pomegranate Banana Yogurt

Serving: 1

Total time: 5 minutes

Ingredients:

- Pomegranate – 2 tablespoons

- Yogurt – ½ cup

- Banana (sliced) – ½

- Hemp seed – 1 heaping spoon

- Unsweetened coconut – 2 tablespoons

- Peanut butter – 1 tablespoon

- Granola – 1 tablespoon

Instructions:

- Combine all the ingredients together in a bowl, then serve.

3.Kiwi and Mango yogurt

Serving: 1

Total time: 5 minutes

Ingredients:

- Kiwi (1/2 inch cubes) – ½ cup

- Mango (1/2inch cubes) – ½ cup

- Yogurt – ½ cup

Instructions:

- Combine all the ingredients together in a bowl.

- Serve.

4.Pumpkin Pie Yogurt and Chocolate

Serving: 1

Total time: 5 minutes

Ingredients:

- Pumpkin pie yogurt- 1/2 cup

- Chocolate Chex™ cereal (crushed) – ¼ cup

- Semisweet chocolate chip – 2 teaspoons

- Frozen whipped cream – 2 tablespoons

Instructions:

- Add half of yogurt in the bottom of glass, then add cereal and chocolate chip, pour the remaining yogurt and top with frozen whipped cream.

- Serve.

5.Avocado Yogurt

Serving: 1

Total time: 5 minutes

Ingredients:

- Yogurt – ¼ cup

- Avocado (cut into cubes) – 1

Instructions:

- Pour the yogurt to avocado cubes in a glass or a bowl.

- Serve.

6.Honey Peach Yogurt

Serving: 1

Total time: 10 minutes

Ingredients:

- Honey – 4 tablespoons

- Peach – 4 cups

- Plain yogurt – ½ cup

- Lemon juice – 1 tablespoon

- Slice of lemon – 1 (for garnish)

Instructions:

- Combine yogurt, honey, peach and lemon juice in a blender or a food processor, press the button and let the mixture gets creamy (about 5 minutes).

- Pour the mixture in a glass and serve.

Chapter 13. Smoothies

Smoothie is often easy to make, within 5 – 10 minutes you already have a glass of delicious and creamy smoothie that is healthy and full of energy, so that's why smoothies are choices for breakfast of women in the busy mornings before going to work.

1.Spinach and Kiwi Smoothie

Serving: 2

Total time:

Ingredients:

- Baby spinach – 1 cup

- Kiwi (peeled) – 2

- Banana – ½

- Yogurt – ½ cup

- Ground flax seed – 2 tablespoons

- Apple juice – ½ cup

- Ice cube - 10

Instructions:

- Put all the ingredients in a blender or food processor, press the button.

- When it's ready, pour it in 2 glasses and serve.

2.Raspberry, Strawberry and Blueberry Smoothie

Serving: 3 - 4

Total time: 10 minutes

Ingredients:

- Raspberry – 1 cup

- Strawberry – 1 cup

- Blueberry – ½ cup

- Water – ¼ cup

- Honey – 2 tablespoons

- Cottage cheese – ½ cup

- Ice cube – 12 cubes.

Instructions:

- Put all the ingredients in a food processor or a blender, then press the button the get your smooth mixture.

- Pour it in a glass, and serve.

3.Beet, Raspberry, Strawberry and Mango Smoothie

Serving: 4

Total time: 15 minutes

Ingredients:

- Beet (peeled and shredded) – 1 cup

- Raspberry – 1 cup

- Strawberry (sliced) – 1 cup

- Mango (cut into chunks) – 1 cup

- Pineapple (cut into chunks) – 1 cup

- Avocado – 1

- Banana – 2

- Vanilla – 2 teaspoons

Instructions:

- Put all the ingredients in a blender, then press the button to mix them well.

- When the mixture is smooth, pour in 4 glasses, then serve.

4.Kale and Spinach Smoothie

Serving: 4

Total time: 10 minutes

Ingredients:

- Kale – 1 cup

- Baby spinach – 1 cup

- Pineapple (diced) – 1 cup

- Banana – ½

- Cottage cheese – ½ cup

- Honey – 2 tablespoons

- Ice cube – 12 cubes

Instructions:

- Put all the ingredients in a blender or a food processor, press the button and let all ingredients mix well.

- Pour in a glass and serve.

5.Peach and Mango Smoothie

Serving: 2 - 3

Total time: 10 minutes

Ingredients:

- Peach (diced) – 1 cup

- Mango (diced) – 1 cup

- Water – ¼ cup

- Cottage cheese – ½ cup

- Honey – 2 teaspoons

- Ice cube – 10 cubes

Instructions:

- Put all the ingredients including peach, mango, water, honey, cheese and ice cubes in a blender.

- Mix them well until smooth.

- Serve.

6.Very Simple and Quick Avocado Smoothie

Serving: 1

Total time: 7 minutes

Ingredients:

- Avocado (cut into cubes) - 2

- Milk – ½ cup

- Sugar – 2 tablespoons

- Ice cube – 4 cubes

Instructions:

- Add avocado, ice cubes, sugar and milk in a food processor.

- Mix them well until smooth.

- Pour the mixture in a glass and serve.

Chapter 14. Drinks

All you know that during pregnancy you are required to stay hydrated all the time. Also, you are recommended to get enough all vitamins. Therefore, how amazing it is when you can quench your thirst and you can prevent you from vitamin deficiency and dehydration at the same time.

1.Ginger, Apple and Carrot Juice

Serving: 2

Total time: 15 minutes

Ingredients:

- Ginger – ½ inch piece

- Apple (peeled and cut into small pieces) – 4

- Carrot (peeled and cut into small pieces) – 4

- Lemon juice – 2 tablespoons

- Sugar – 2 tablespoons

Instructions:

- Put the first three ingredients in a food processor.

- Then pour it into a sieve to strain the liquid.

- Add sugar and lemon juice to the juice.

- Serve.

2.Orange Juice

Serving: 4

Total time: 15 minutes

Ingredients:

- Frozen orange juice concentrate – 6 ounces

- Water – 1cup

- Milk – 1 cup

- Granulated sugar – ½ cup

- Vanilla – 1 teaspoon

- Ice cube – 1 cup

Instructions:

- Put all the ingredients in a food processor or a blender.

- Press the button and let they are blended well.

- Pour in four glasses

- Serve.

3.Carrot, Lemon and Pineapple

Serving: 2 - 3

Total time: 15 minutes

Ingredients

- Pineapple – ½ cup

- Strawberry – ½ cup

- Orange (cut into segments) – ½ cup

- Carrot (1/4 inch chunks) – 1

- Lemon juice – 1 tablespoon

- Almond milk – ½ cup

- Ice cube – 10

Instructions:

- Add 7 ingredients into a blender.

- Mix them well.

- Enjoy.

4.Easy Lemonade Juice

Serving: 1

Total time: 10 minutes

Ingredients:

- Lemon – 2

- Water – ¼ cup

- Sugar – 2 tablespoons

- Ice cube – 6 cubes

Instructions:

- Halve the lemons, and remove seeds.

- Using a juicer to get the lemon juice.

- Combine lemon juice, ice cube and sugar in a blender, then mix them well.

- Serve.

5.Coconut Water Calamansi Juice

Serving: 1

Total time: 10 minutes

Ingredients:

- Young coconut - 1

- Calamansi – 1

- Sugar – 2 teaspoons

- Ice cube – 5 cubes

Instructions:

- Extract the Calamansi juice.

- Blend all the ingredients together and mix them well.

- Serve.

Note. Calamansi is a citrus fruit that has the same family as lime, but it's tartness isn't so sharp as lime and it gives you a great flavor when pairing with coconut water. However, in case, you can't find any Calamansi around, it is still ok to pair with lime or lemon but just use about one wedge of lemon for 1 coconut. Give it a try and enjoy how amazing it is!

6.Lemonade Blueberry

Serving: 2

Total time: 15 minutes

Ingredients:

- Lemon juice – 5

- Water – 1 ½ cups

- Blueberry – ½ cups

For the syrup

- Water – ½ cup

- Sugar – ½ cup

Instructions:

- Mix water and sugar, and heat it until the sugar is dissolved to make the syrup.

- Mix 1 ½ cups of water with lemon juice in a pitcher.

- Add the syrup into the pitcher and stir well.

- Add the blueberry into the pitcher, use a fork to mash up the blueberry.

- Serve.

Chapter 15. Recipes for Vegetarians

If you are tired of eating fishes, meat and poultry meal by meal and day by day, think of recipes for vegetarians instead. Because most of the recipes consist largely of vegetables or fruits which mean no meat or fish used in them, they are very healthy and nutritious. However, all of the ingredients in these recipes are not 100% of vegetables, cereal and fruits, there are still some ingredients that are derived from animals like eggs and cheese, which strict vegans may be a little disappointed.

1.Grilled Pineapple

Serving: 2

Total time: 30 minutes

Ingredients:

- Whole pineapple (cut into 1 inch spears) – 1

- Red onion – ½ cup

- Cilantro (chopped) – ¼ cup

- Pepper (chopped) – 1

- Lime juice – 2 tablespoons

- Olive oil – 3 tablespoons

Instructions:

- Preheat your grill over high medium heat.

- Place the pineapple and grill for 5 – 10 minutes. Then remove from the grill.

- Mix all the ingredients together, gently toss to coat.

- Keep it in refrigerator.

2.Avocado Toast with Kale

Serving: 2

Total time: 30 minutes

Ingredients:

- Kale – 1 cup

- Lemon – ½

- Avocado – 4 ounces

- Olive oil – 1 teaspoon

- Bread – 4 slices

- Cumin – 1/8 teaspoon

- Radish (sliced) – 4 slices

- Chia seeds – 1 teaspoon

- Salt and pepper

Instructions:

- In a bowl, add kale, olive oil, lemon juice and a little salt and mix them well.

- Halve the avocado. Cut into slices one of them. And smash the other. Season the smash avocado with a little salt, pepper and lemon juice.

- Toast the slices of bread

- Spread the smashed avocado on the toasted bread slices, then place slices of avocado on top and sprinkle a little salt, pepper and cumin.

- Place the mixture of kale, radish and chia seeds on top of bread. And serve.

3.Baked Squash Blossom

Serving: 2

Total time: 30 minutes

Ingredients:

- Squash blossom – 12

- Ricotta – 1 cup

- Egg (divided) – 3

- Parsley – 1/3 cup

- Breadcrumb – ¾ cup

- Salt – 1 teaspoon

Instructions:

- Preheat the oven to 400 degrees.

- Combine 1 egg, ricotta, parsley and a little salt well together. Mix them well.

- Crack the remaining eggs, and beat them well in a bowl.

- Filling the squash blossoms with the mixture of ricotta and egg.

- Then dip the stuffed squash blossoms in egg, breadcrumbs, then place them on baking sheet lined with parchment paper, then bake for 10 minutes.

Note: Instead of baking, you can make them fried in oil.

4.Fried Apple

Serving: 1

Total time: 25 minutes.

Ingredients:

- Apple (cut into cubes or thick slices) – 2 large

- Butter (chopped) – 4 tablespoons

- White sugar – 2 tablespoons

- Brown sugar – 2 tablespoons

- Lemon juice – ½

- Cinnamon – 1 teaspoon

Instructions:

- Heat the skillet and let the butter melted.

- Add the apple, stir and add lemon juice into the skillet, cook until the apples are tender.

- Add sugar and stir well to coat evenly the apples.

- Add cinnamon to the apples, toss to coat.

- Remove from heat. Serve.

5.Spinach with Sesame Oil

Serving: 2

Total time: 30 minutes

Ingredients:

- Spinach – 8 ounces

- Sesame oil – 1 ½ teaspoons

- Sesame seed – 2 teaspoons

- Soy sauce – 1 ½ teaspoons

- Green onion (chopped) – 1

- Garlic (minced) – 1 clove

Instructions:

- Blanch the spinach in hot water for 30 second, remove and place in very cold water.

- Let the spinach drained, and squeeze out the excess water.

- Mix the spinach with other ingredients including sesame oil, soy sauce, sesame seeds, minced garlic and green onion together.

- Serve.

6.Spinach and Cheese Cups

Serving: 3

Total time: 25 minutes

Ingredients:

- Spinach (chopped) – 1 cup

- Shredded Cheddar Cheese – 1 cup

- Egg – 12

- Onion powder – 2 teaspoons

- Salt and pepper

Instructions:

- Preheat the oven to 400 degrees

- Break eggs and place in a bowl then add cheese, chopped spinach, eggs and onion powder and season with salt and pepper.

- Brush oil on the bottom of muffin tins then pour the mixture into them, about 12 cups. Cook for 10 minutes.

- Remove and serve

Conclusion

Pregnancy time is a special time when everything in life seems to change including the way you eat and what you eat. During this time, you aren't eating for not only yourself but also the baby and, of course, a healthy baby will be born to a mother who consumes a lot of healthy foods. Therefore, there is no better way to get all the essential nutrients by creating a well-balanced diet during 9 months of pregnancy. But what a well-balance diet should be? It must be high in vitamins and minerals but minimize the unhealthy substances. Plus, the ingredients in each recipe must be fresh and high quality, so low-fat products and organic vegetables must be a priority. Therefore, I hope that with the 90 recipes contained in this cookbook, you will have a great collection of healthy recipes that is easy to follow at home. Moreover, for those who are busy won't feel lazy to spend at least 10 − 30 minutes to prepare a meal for yourself. Plus, I hope that these recipes will fit even the pickiest eaters' taste.

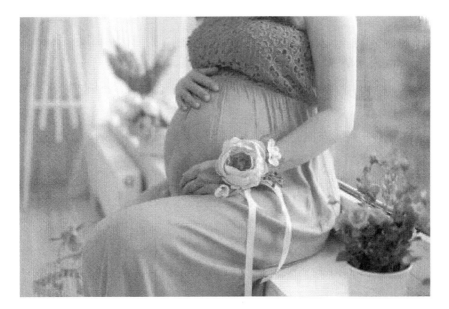

- [Melanie]

ABOUT THE AUTHOR

Hi, everybody! My name is Melanie and 28 years old. As a regular woman, I love the normal things like other regular people like. I love music, shopping, travelling, cooking and eating. As an eating lover luckily I'm not a picky eater. I can eat mostly everything and I must confess that I'm a big fan of coffee and my breakfast is always paired with a cup of coffee. To me food doesn't the thing that keep us survived it also has its own story which can be associated with the culture of where it is come from or the way it was invented or how it affects to health, so each new food I try to cook or eat makes me fascinated to learn the stories behind.

There are a few things that I would consider my first priority in life. They are my family, friends and career, so everything I do in life would be around these. I also witnessed the death of my uncle after having a long battle against his diabetes. Before that he had had to follow a strict diet and had to ignore a lot of great foods he liked because they are high in sugar, which sometimes bothered him a lot. I also have an aunt who isn't allowed to drink coffee and soya products by doctors due to having been diagnosed with hyperthyroidism. Therefore I understand that health is the key for everything. I mean that we can't enjoy all excitements in life without health, so everything can give me healthier is worth learning and trying, so food is a part of them.

And for those reasons my two books were written. Yeap, that's right! My two books are born with an ambition to remind everybody to pay more attention to what we eat, particularly in these two books, I give my priority to the health of women who are pregnant – the most beautiful time in life but also the vulnerable time they have to experience. Hope that with my two books I somewhat help the readers have not only basic knowledge about the importance of nutrition during pregnancy but also have great meals to eat in order to survive and to eat to be healthier.

Made in the USA
Columbia, SC
02 January 2019